First World War
and Army of Occupation
War Diary
France, Belgium and Germany

55 DIVISION
164 Infantry Brigade,
Brigade Trench Mortar Battery
1 August 1916 - 2 August 1916

WO95/2924/3

The Naval & Military Press Ltd
www.nmarchive.com
Published in association with The National Archives

Published by

The Naval & Military Press Ltd

Unit 10 Ridgewood Industrial Park,

Uckfield, East Sussex,

TN22 5QE England

Tel: +44 (0) 1825 749494

www.naval-military-press.com

www.nmarchive.com

This diary has been reprinted in facsimile from the original. Any imperfections are inevitably reproduced and the quality may fall short of modern type and cartographic standards.

© **Crown Copyright**
Images reproduced by permission of The National Archives, London, England, 2015.

Contents

Document type	Place/Title	Date From	Date To
Heading	WO95/2924-3		
Heading	55th Division 164th Infy Bde 164th Trench Mortar Bty Aug 1916		
Heading	War Diary Of 164th Trench Mortar Battery From 1st To 31st August 1916 Vol 1		
War Diary	Trenches	01/08/1916	09/08/1916
War Diary	Bivouac Bronfay Farm	10/08/1916	14/08/1916
War Diary	Billets at Mericourt	15/08/1916	19/08/1916
War Diary	Billets Campagne	20/08/1916	23/08/1916
War Diary	Cayeux	24/08/1916	26/08/1916
War Diary	Billets Campagne	27/08/1916	29/08/1916
War Diary	Le Toquet	30/08/1916	30/08/1916
War Diary	Camp Albert Amiens Mont	31/08/1916	31/08/1916
War Diary	Trenches	02/08/1916	02/08/1916

WO 95/29244 (3)

WO 95/29244 (3)

55TH DIVISION
164TH INFY BDE

164TH TRENCH MORTAR BTY

AUG 1916

Confidential

War Diary

of

164th Trench Mortar Battery

From 1st to 31st August 1916

WAR DIARY or INTELLIGENCE SUMMARY

Army Form C. 2118.

(Erase heading not required.)

Instructions regarding War Diaries and Intelligence Summaries are contained in F.S. Regs., Part II. and the Staff Manual respectively. Title pages will be prepared in manuscript.

Place	Date	Hour	Summary of Events and Information	Remarks and references to Appendices
Trenches	1/8/16		2 Detachments and Mortars in positions at Crour Head Chez and Molly Hans Farm with 1/4th Kingston Royal Scots Regt. 2 Detachments and Mortars in positions in front of Trones Wood with 1/8th (Irish) Kings Liverpool Regt. 4 detachments with Mortars in reserve with 1/4th Loyal North Lancs Regt. Dublin Trench. Consolidating positions and continuing ammunition dumps. Casualties Nil.	
	2/8/16		Continuing ammunition dumps, preparing, and carrying ammunition up to the trench. Casualties 2 O.R. Reference situation See Sketch attached.	
	3/8/16		Preparing ammunition, and carrying up to the trench. Casualties 2 O.R.	
	4/9/16		Preparing ammunition, and carrying. Casualties 16 O.R. Operations: Bombed enemy strong point on Guillemont Station Road, about 140 rounds rapid fire, were dropped into enemy's position. The enemy front was then stormed and captured by a platoon of the 1/4th Loyal North Lancs, at the cost of only 3 casualties O.R. It was afterwards consolidated and held by a platoon of the 1/5th Kings Liverpool Regt 165th Infantry Brigade.	
	5/8/16			
	6/8/16		Preparing and carrying ammunition up to the line, and continued work Butties and Preparing and carrying of Ammunition. Casualties 1 O.R.	

WAR DIARY
or
INTELLIGENCE SUMMARY
(Erase heading not required.)

Army Form C. 2118
3

Place	Date	Hour	Summary of Events and Information	Remarks and references to Appendices
Trenches	7/8/16		Preparing and carrying ammunition. Centred ammunition dump about 5 enemy shells and shrapnel cup. About 1500 rounds of ammunition destroyed in explosion.	
	8/8/16	4.15 a.m	and the 10A Brigade attack. Object to capture village of Guillemont and consolidate on far side of village. Stokes Mortars to advance as soon as possible after first infantry wave, and assist in holding and consolidating captured positions, [?] to co-operate [?] and clearing enemy strong points and advanced positions. At 3 a.m. No.1 detachment laid out position in shell holes at S24 d 68 immediately to the right of Arrowhead and Guillemont Sunken Road. No. 2 detachment occupied shell hole at S30 b 51 close to Potsdam trench. No.3 detachment and No.4 detachment were placed in reserve - positions at S24 d 10 & S24 d 0 6 Potsdam Trench. Ammunition had previously been carried to these positions during the night 7/8/16. No.2 section with Arrows early held in reserve with supports positions Col B 35 a.m. No. 1 & 2 arrows found enemy shrapnel on front of Sunken Road & Pistols [?] the road behind the ground. About 250 rounds were fired during that engagement [?]. At 4.25a.m received message that 1/4 Royal Highl. observation of fire was difficult. At 4.25a.m received message that 1/4 Royal [?] [?] the 1/4 up in every way in front of enemy advanced trench [?], no our trench trenches for our hospital was a little further to the near the crest of hill. No.1 & 2 sections are all over hospital. While searching for available positions for Arrows to open fire to right - rear direction. the 1/4 Royal Guns Highl. were seen to retire, being forced back by the enemy [?]. The Arrows were placed in shell holes close to Potsdam trench capable of [?] of energy fire. The difficulty of selecting suitable supply of ammunition, but was controlled and [?] every [?], [?] on our enemy counter attacks, if any.	Ref. Map [?] Guillemont Scale 1/20,000 Corrected 25.20/7/16

1875 Wt. W593/826 1,000,000 4/15 J.B.C. & A. A.D.S.S./Forms/C. 2118.

Army Form C. 2118

WAR DIARY
or
INTELLIGENCE SUMMARY
(Erase heading not required.)

Instructions regarding War Diaries and Intelligence Summaries are contained in F. S. Regs., Part II. and the Staff Manual respectively. Title Pages will be prepared in manuscript.

4

Place	Date	Hour	Summary of Events and Information	Remarks and references to Appendices
Trônes	8/8/16	2pm	At noon 2nd Lieut Johnson who had the taken over command of 1/14 London Regt instructed us to fire on enemy strong point 330 t 73 (Sunken Road) Lieut Coe rescinds were found into the position. When it was found impossible to proceed we commenced coming a very heavy shell fire, shell not attached. The four guns under command were knocked up to accompany the infantry had been elected & forced to return. They were placed in position on the right flank to cover the sunken road and entrenchment north of the 1/6th Queens Regt & 1/5 Cheshires Regt and took up position in shell holes at S24 d 29 & S24 d 41 approximately at about 4.30 a.m. The officer in command 2nd Lieut J.A.H. Coates was apparently left while conducting a carrying party with ammunition & have advanced position. It was found impossible to get ammunition forward owing to enemy barrage and Mr Guns fire. The men are seen throwing rifle bombs on the enemy 8/9 d 8 & 9/4 occupied north of Lance Reserve Regt having been forced to return. Casualties: 2nd Lieut J.A.H. Coates (Recovery Returned). Killed) O.R. 2 killed (Somers), wounded killed, wounded	Ref Map Guillemont Scale 1/10000
			Prob. 20-30 - Preparing enlarging commutations. About 160 received information that the 166 infantry Brigade would attack at dawn. No 152 trenches were placed in position at S30 d 65 & S30 d 51. No 754 & S24 d 10 & S24 d 56, No 6,57 was placed protecting at S30 a 66 & S30 d 44 rather better than previous in shell holes to the left of sunken trench at S30 a 44 to the right and the 1/5 Loyal North Lancashire on right flank. About 4.20 10th Scottish & L.N.L. made on Guillemont which they over ran & 1. on the retirement of Lance Fusiliers, counted as sketch on Guillemont held	28/8/16
	9/8/16			

Army Form C. 2118

WAR DIARY
or
INTELLIGENCE SUMMARY

(Erase heading not required.)

Instructions regarding War Diaries and Intelligence Summaries are contained in F. S. Regs., Part II. and the Staff Manual respectively. Title Pages will be prepared in manuscript.

Place	Date	Hour	Summary of Events and Information	Remarks and references to Appendices
Trenches	9/8/16 Continued		Sf the 1st Scottish R.L.I., these opened on the trench up to [illegible] there for a barrage over center of [illegible] blew [illegible] were visible. About 300 rounds were fired, it deliberate and rapid fire being employed. The enemy did not counter attack. We were compelled to cease fire owing to lack of ammunition at the mortar positions at 10 a.m. As the battery was relieved and went out to William Redt. At noon proceeded to Rendezvous at Bonfay Farm, when the battery bivouaced. Casualties O.R.s 1 killed, 6 wounded. Destroyed 1 mortar, destroyed 3 shell pits.	
Bonfay Farm	10/5/16		Rest. Battery inspected by Major General Jackson. Reinforcements 3 O.R.s Casualties nil	
"	11/8/16		Battery refitting and training. Casualties nil	
"	12/8/16		Battery having [illegible] Casualties nil.	
"	13/8/16		Battery training. Casualties nil.	
"	14/8/16		Battery training. Casualties nil.	
"			Route March to Mericourt, arrived 8.15 p.m. 6 mortars elsewhere taken up to Albert. School of Battery. Casualties nil.	
Billets at Mericourt	16/8/16		Battery training. Billets inspected by Brigadier General Phillips. Casualties nil.	
"	16/8/16		Battery training. Casualties nil.	

WAR DIARY
or
INTELLIGENCE SUMMARY
(Erase heading not required.)

Army Form C. 2118

Instructions regarding War Diaries and Intelligence Summaries are contained in F. S. Regs., Part II. and the Staff Manual respectively. Title Pages will be prepared in manuscript.

Place	Date	Hour	Summary of Events and Information	Remarks and references to Appendices
Ouillet Huonval	17/8/16		Battery Training Casualties Nil	
	18/8/16		Battery Training Casualties Nil	
	19/8/16		Entrained at Huonval for Campagne nr. Pont-Remy Casualties Nil	
Billets Campagne	20/8/16		Wrote over to Pont Remy & Campagne Chard Bivouacs and Stables Casualties Nil	
	21/8/16		Training Casualties Nil	
	22/8/16		Training Casualties Nil	
	23/8/16		Battery left at 7.92 am & was taken to Cayeux. Route march to Port & Grand Casualties Nil	
			Battery Bivd & Grand Van and G.H. Lorne Wagons 730 f. --	
Cayeux	24/8/16		Bathing on Sea Casualties Nil	
	25/8/16		Battery on Sea Casualties Nil	
	26/8/16		Return at Cayeux 12+7 and 8f -- Lorne Packages 8f -- Casualties Nil	
Billets Campagne	27/8/16		Sent Guards Casualties Nil	
	28/8/16		Training Casualties Nil	
	29/8/16		Training 6.30 pm left for Le Joyard & rode march 2.15 a.m. Between at Pont Remy 5.30 a.m.	
Le Joyard	30/8/16		Detrain at Pont Remy by rode march 7.30 a.m. Arrived army & trough at D. Bof 25 by 13 h 92 y. Petamunel-If-Arthur	
			Gun Positions about 7.30 am. Casualties and Reinforcements 2nd Lieut. O. Lynch 90A -- up 9.40 am.)	
			Bivouaced. Heavy rains. Casualties Nil	
Courcelles-au-Bois	31/8/16		Training Casualties Nil	

F. P. Bristol Capt.
O.C. 164 Siege Battery Canadian

31/8/16

WAR DIARY or INTELLIGENCE SUMMARY

Army Form C. 2118

Place	Date	Hour	Summary of Events and Information	Remarks and references to Appendices
Flanders	2/6/16		About 6 p.m. the O.C. 1/4th Kings Own R. Lancs Regt. instructed us to dig 2 or 3 new front trenches the enemy had taken up and were consolidating just below the crest of the hill and to the left front of the Wytham Farm. Three bombers were placed in positions to command the objective. About 8.30 p.m. Nos 1 & 2 in front of 40 rounds of rapid and 3 & 4 of 35 & 40 rounds were seen to B.O.H. Some ten minutes later 40 some time it appeared that 1/6 (L. North Lancs) coys next of ourselves on the right flank. A party of the Battalion about 80 strong were endeavouring to reach the sunken road, when some 60 or 80 germans emerged from an advanced trench on their right and advanced to the attack. The three bombers were sufficient and enfiladed this opened on the advancing enemy. The firing appeared to be effective. A number of germans were seen who it was believed were the enemy. At another enemy machine gun to leave guns put from the left somewhere, opened. The enemy front which had been furiously bombed was stormed and captured by the 1/4th Kings Own Regt. have kept their trenches clear sight. The enemy from where name not once a heavy heavy on trench hard.	

J.J. Godd? Capt?
O.C. 164 T.M. Batty

www.ingramcontent.com/pod-product-compliance
Lightning Source LLC
Chambersburg PA
CBHW081513160426
43193CB00014B/2679